Pet Pals

Pet Guinea Pigs

Julia Barnes

GARETH**STEVENS**
PUBLISHING

A Member of the WRC Media Family of Companies

Please visit our web site at: www.garethstevens.com
For a free color catalog describing Gareth Stevens Publishing's
list of high-quality books and multimedia programs, call
1-800-542-2595 (USA) or 1-800-387-3178 (Canada).
Gareth Stevens Publishing's fax: (414) 332-3567.

Library of Congress Cataloging-in-Publication Data

Barnes, Julia, 1955-
    Pet guinea pigs / Julia Barnes. — North American ed.
        p. cm. — (Pet pals)
    Includes bibliographical references and index.
    ISBN-10: 0-8368-6779-3 — ISBN-13: 978-0-8368-6779-4 (lib. bdg.)
    1. Guinea pigs as pets—Juvenile literature. I. Title.
    SF459.G9B3755   2007
    636.935'92—dc22   2006042373

This edition first published in 2007 by
Gareth Stevens Publishing
A Member of the WRC Media Family of Companies
330 West Olive Street, Suite 100
Milwaukee, Wisconsin 53212 USA

This U.S. edition copyright © 2007 by Gareth Stevens, Inc.
Original edition copyright © 2007 by Westline Publishing,
P.O. Box 8, Lydney, Gloucestershire, GL15 6YD, United Kingdom.

Gareth Stevens series editor: Leifa Butrick
Gareth Stevens cover design: Dave Kowalski
Gareth Stevens art direction: Tammy West

Picture Credits:
Oxford Scientific, pp. 4 (Alan and Sandy Carey),
6 (Paul Franklin); Tony Northrup (www.northrup.org),
p. 19; Andy Gray (www.japanwindow.com), p. 22.
All other images copyright © 2007 Westline Publishing.
Thanks to Joanna Smith for help with picture research.

Printed in the United States of America

1 2 3 4 5 6 7 8 9 10 09 08 07 06

Cover: Guinea pigs love to explore secret tunnels.

Contents

Words that appear in the glossary are printed in
boldface type the first time they occur in the text.

In the Wild

The first guinea pigs lived in Peru, a country in South America.

Guinea pigs are members of the **rodent** family, which includes mice, rats, and hamsters. It is the largest group of **mammals** on Earth. Rodents can look very different from each other, but they all share one feature. Each rodent has four big front teeth — two on the top and two on the bottom — which the rodent uses for gnawing. The family name "rodent" comes from the Latin word *rodere*, which means "to gnaw." A guinea pig's front teeth, or **incisors**, grow throughout the animal's life.

The Hunted

Guinea pigs are also called **cavies**, which is the name that breeders and other experts prefer to use. The wild **ancestor** of the guinea pig is the *Cavia cutleri*, which means "restless cavy." Wild cavies still live in South America. In the wild, guinea pigs **graze** on grass and plants, but they must always be on the lookout for meat-eating

The wild cavy lives on open grasslands and has to be watchful.

Like their wild ancestors, guinea pigs produce young that are very advanced at birth. These piglets are only ten days old.

predators that are looking for a quick meal. Living in constant danger makes wild cavies nervous and fast-moving, and pet guinea pigs also show this behavior.

Family Life

Sometimes, wild cavies use burrows left by other animals, but most of the time, wild cavies live in the open. Usually, between five and ten cavies form a group. A group has one male, called a **boar**; several females, called **sows**; and their babies, known as piglets.

Most small mammals give birth to their young in nests. Their babies are born blind, have no fur, and rely on their mothers to feed them. Cavies, however, give birth in the open, so their babies have to be ready to look after themselves almost from the day they are born. For this reason, guinea pig babies are very advanced at birth.

- They are born with their eyes open.
- They are large, weighing about 2 ounces (57 grams). A full-grown cavy weighs about 2 pounds (907 g).
- They have full coats of fur.
- They have all their teeth.
- Within a few days, they can eat solid food.

Cavy Care

In order to produce well-developed babies, a female cavy has a long **pregnancy** lasting sixty-three days. By comparison, a female hamster is pregnant for just sixteen days.

The Human Link

People in South America brought cavies in from the wild and used them as food.

The **Incas** of Peru first caught guinea pigs in the wild about 5000 B.C. They used the animals for food but kept them like pets. Guinea pigs were allowed to run around the floors of the Incas' homes and were fed table scraps.

On special occasions, the Incas **sacrificed** guinea pigs as part of religious ceremonies — and then ate them. The Incas had a constant supply of guinea pigs, because they kept the animals in enclosed areas and allowed them to breed.

Guinea pigs are sociable animals and are happy living in large groups.

Guinea pigs have become popular pets.

European Soldiers

Spanish soldiers who invaded Peru in the fifteenth century liked the Incas' guinea pigs. When the soldiers returned to Europe, they took guinea pigs with them to eat on the journey. The guinea pigs that did not become a meal went to Spain as pets.

The people in Spain were delighted with the charming little animals, and ever since then, people have kept guinea pigs as pets in both Spain and Portugal. News about guinea pigs spread. Soon, people in other European countries also kept them as pets.

In those days, guinea pigs were expensive, so only rich families could afford them. Elizabeth I, who was queen of England from 1558 to 1603, owned several pet guinea pigs.

What Is in a Name?

When a guinea pig was prepared for a meal, the roasted animal looked like a little pig. The Spanish gave it the name *cochinillo*, which means "little pig."

No one knows how or why the word *guinea* became part of the name. Perhaps when guinea pigs were first sold in Europe as pets, the animals cost one guinea (about $1.80) — a lot of money in those days. Perhaps people had the mistaken idea that the animals came from Guinea, a country in Africa.

Did you know?

Guinea pigs are still a source of food in South America. In Peru, Bolivia, and Ecuador, roast guinea pig is a popular dish.

Perfect Pets

Guinea pigs are one of the most popular small animals to keep as pets.

uinea pigs make wonderful pets for many reasons.

- Guinea pigs are gentle creatures that rarely bite or scratch.
- Guinea pigs are larger than many other small pets, such as hamsters and gerbils, so guinea pigs are easier to handle.

- Guinea pigs are active during the day, so they are awake when their owners are, and they sleep when their owners sleep. Some small animals are active mostly at night.
- Guinea pigs have few health problems if their owners look after them properly.
- Guinea pigs live for about six years, which is longer than other small pets.

Over time, you can build a close relationship with a guinea pig.

- People who are **allergic** to pets with fur can still keep guinea pigs if the animals can stay in an outdoor hutch. Doctors can test people for pet allergies.

A Guinea Pig's Needs

Do not rush out to buy a guinea pig because you think it will be an easy pet to take care of. Like all living creatures, guinea pigs have specific needs.

- Guinea pigs will be unhappy living alone, so plan to keep more than one.
- Guinea pigs need secure, comfortable housing with enough room to move around.

- A guinea pig's hutch or cage needs to be kept clean.
- Long-haired guinea pigs need grooming.
- A guinea pig's teeth must be filed and its nails cut, if they grow too long.
- A guinea pig needs someone to take care of it, if its owner goes away for more than a day.
- Guinea pigs like to run and play, so they need outdoor runs or indoor playpens.

A guinea pig is a curious animal and is interested in everything that is going on.

A Guinea Pig's Body

Guinea pigs have some unusual features that make them different from other animals.

Eyes
A guinea pig can see in front and to the side without moving its head, which helps the guinea pig spot predators in the wild. A guinea pig is good at seeing sudden movements, and it can see **primary colors**, such as red, blue, and green, but its vision is not as good as a human being's.

Nose
A guinea pig has a good sense of smell. It can recognize other guinea pigs by smell and will also get to know the smell of its owner. Guinea pigs choose food by smell, too. Their noses help them avoid poisonous plants.

Teeth
A guinea pig's teeth grow all the time. It has twenty teeth in its mouth. Its four incisors are just behind the lips.

Front Feet
Each front foot has four claws.

Ears

A guinea pig has bald spots behind its ears. Depending on the kind of guinea pig, the ears are small and upright or large and rose-shaped or drooping. A guinea pig's sense of hearing is twice as powerful as a human's.

Whiskers

A guinea pig uses its sensitive whiskers to find its way around in the dark. Its whiskers help the guinea pig figure out if it can fit into a particular space.

Coat

Guinea pigs have many different kinds of coats — long, short, curly, rough, or satin. Their coats may be all one color or a mixture of colors. Some coats also have special markings.

Body

A guinea pig's body is short and compact.

Back Feet

Each back foot has three claws.

Tail

A guinea pig's tail is so short that it does not stick out from the animal's body. A guinea pig has eight tailbones that can be felt under the skin.

Cavy Varieties

Coat types, colors, and markings separate guinea pig breeds.

Guinea pigs are popular pets, but many people also enjoy breeding and showing **purebred** cavies. All breeds started as the small, brown guinea pig from South America, but breeders have developed guinea pigs that look very different from their wild ancestors.

Coat Types
Guinea pigs can have several kinds of coats.

- **Smooth:** The English, American, and Bolivian varieties have short, smooth coats that lie flat. Short-haired guinea pigs are the most common type. Short-haired breeds need to be brushed only once a week.

- **Long-haired:** Guinea pigs such as the Peruvian and the Sheltie have such long coats it is sometimes difficult to see the shape of the guinea pig underneath all the hair.

This Dutch red guinea pig has a short, smooth coat that is easy to look after.

The Abyssinian is the only guinea pig with a rough coat.

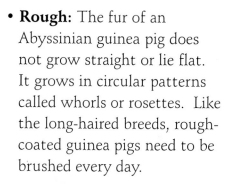

• **Rough:** The fur of an Abyssinian guinea pig does not grow straight or lie flat. It grows in circular patterns called whorls or rosettes. Like the long-haired breeds, rough-coated guinea pigs need to be brushed every day.

Cavy Care

There are many **crossbred** guinea pigs, which come in lots of colors and coat types. Crossbred guinea pigs are not exhibited in the show ring, but they make excellent pets.

This guinea pig has long hair. Guinea pig hair is more like human hair than like rabbit fur and needs regular brushing.

This short-haired guinea pig has a flat crown. Some crowns are rosettes.

- **Rex:** The coat of a Rex guinea pig is woolly and stands straight up like velvet.
- **Crowned:** The crowned guinea pig has a patch of hair growing on the top of its head. This "crown" may be the same color as the rest of the coat, or it may be a different color.
- **Satin:** A guinea pig that has a fine, silky coat with a beautiful shine to the coat is called a satin guinea pig.

Colors

Guinea pigs are either **self-colored** or **marked**.

Self-colored

A guinea pig that is all one color is called "self-colored." It is a smooth-haired animal and could be one of many colors.

- White
- Cream
- Golden — yellowish brown
- Black
- Chocolate
- Red — reddish-brown
- Beige
- Lilac — pale beige or gray

A sable guinea pig is an exotic variety with chocolate-colored hair on its back that becomes a cream color on its sides and belly.

This self-colored guinea pig has a lilac coat and pink eyes.

This tortoiseshell and white guinea pig has an Abyssinian coat.

Marked

If a guinea pig has more than one color in its coat, it is called a "marked" guinea pig. Coats can be marked many ways.

- **Dutch:** colored guinea pig with white face markings and a white saddle
- **Tortoiseshell and white:** a mix of reddish brown, black, and white
- **Dalmatian:** spotted with the same markings as a Dalmatian dog

- **Himalayan:** a white body with dark hair around the nose and ears
- **Agouti:** each hair is two colors that create a banded effect. An agouti can be silver, golden, or cinnamon.

Some guinea pigs have dark eyes that are blue, black, or brown. Other guinea pigs have eyes that may be blue or black, but which reflect red light. These guinea pigs are called red-eyed, pink-eyed, or ruby-eyed.

Half the hair on the back of this Peruvian grows toward its head and falls over its face. It is hard to tell which end is which.

Guinea Pig Homes

A guinea pig needs a safe, secure, and comfortable place to live.

Guinea pigs can live outdoors in hutches during mild weather or in warm climates. Like people, guinea pigs prefer temperatures between 65 and 75 °Fahrenheit (18 and 24 °Celsius). In temperatures above 85 °F (29 °C), guinea pigs can suffer from heatstroke. If you plan to keep your guinea pigs in a hutch, follow these guidelines:

• A hutch should be at least 3 feet (90 centimeters) wide, 2 feet (60 cm) deep, and 18 inches (45 cm) high. A bigger hutch is even better.

• A hutch should stand off the ground on legs that are at least 9 inches (23 cm) long to protect the guinea pigs from drafts.

• The guinea pigs will need a sleeping compartment that is separate from the main part of the hutch.

• The wire mesh covering the front of the main part of the hutch must be narrow enough to keep mice and rats from getting inside.

• A hutch should be lined with wood shavings. A layer of newspaper underneath the shavings will add warmth.

A hutch should shelter guinea pigs from direct sunlight.

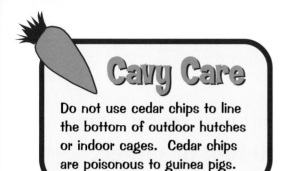

Cavy Care

Do not use cedar chips to line the bottom of outdoor hutches or indoor cages. Cedar chips are poisonous to guinea pigs.

Indoor Cage

Guinea pigs that are kept indoors as house pets need cages that are big enough for them to run around in freely. They also need larger exercise areas, outside the cages, that are safe and secure.

If you plan to keep your guinea pigs indoors, consider these points:

• Although guinea pigs do not like loud noises, you will not have much fun with your pets if you keep them in a cold, quiet, back bedroom. In a living room or family room, guinea pigs will adapt to family sounds, and everyone will be able to enjoy them.

• You can easily build ramps and platforms for your guinea pigs to play on. They also love dark, cozy boxes to hide in.

Bedding

The best type of bedding to use is wood shavings. If you cover the shavings with a layer of hay in the sleeping area, your guinea pigs will stay snug and warm.

Water

Guinea pigs must have fresh water available at all times. Most people attach a water bottle to the side of the hutch or cage.

This indoor cage has a cover to keep the guinea pigs from jumping out.

Playtime

Guinea pigs need places to exercise outside their hutches or cages.

This outside run is lightweight and easy to move around.

Cavy Care

Make sure your guinea pigs have at least one hour-long session a day in their exercise area. In nice weather, the guinea pigs will enjoy staying out for longer periods.

Guinea pigs enjoy spending time outside their hutches, when they are free to run around and eat grass. Most runs for small animals are about 10 feet (3 meters) long, 3 feet (1 m) wide, and are triangular in shape. Chicken wire makes a good roof and sides, but part of the run should have a solid cover so the guinea pigs can rest in the shade or find shelter from rain.

Guinea pigs love to sunbathe, but do not let them overdo it! They have no hair behind their ears, and these bald spots can get sunburned. Remember to move the run to a new place every day so your guinea pigs have fresh grass to eat. Do not forget to attach a water bottle to the run and keep the bottle full.

Treats drop out of an activity ball when a guinea pig pushes it.

Indoor Play Areas

If you keep your guinea pigs in the house, they still need to spend time outside their cages in an exercise area. You can let your guinea pigs run free, but be sure that nothing in the room can hurt them and that your guinea pigs cannot run out of the room. It is safer to use the kind of exercise pens that pet stores sell for small animals, but you can also use a child's playpen. The ideal size playpen for two or three guinea pigs is 3 feet (1 m) by 4 feet (1.2 m). The pen must be escape-proof. A shallow plastic tray filled with wood shavings should cover the base of the pen.

Toys

Guinea pigs do not play with toys the way small pets such as hamsters and gerbils do because they cannot hold toys with their front feet. Guinea pigs, however, love to gnaw, so they like chewable toys. The best type are the hard wooden toys made for parrots. Guinea pigs also like to have hiding places, such as cardboard boxes with cutout holes.

Guinea pigs love to explore secret tunnels.

The Right Choice

Look for signs of a healthy guinea pig.

Coat
A guinea pig's fur should be glossy and clean with no bald patches.

Skin
The skin under a guinea pig's fur should not be flaky or have sores.

Ears
Be sure the ears are clean.

Eyes
Look for bright, clear eyes.

Rear End
If hair around its rear end is matted, the guinea pig could have diarrhea.

Body
A guinea pig's body should be plump, without any bumps or swellings.

Mouth
Signs of drooling could mean tooth problems.

Nostrils
The nostrils should be free of discharge.

If you want purebred guinea pigs, you need to go to a cavy breeder. If you are happy with crossbred guinea pigs, you can buy them at your local pet store. Take a good look around the store first so you know that the animals are kept in clean conditions.

Be sure that the guinea pigs for sale are about six weeks old. Older guinea pigs that are not used to being handled will not bond with a human family.

Male or Female?

The staff at the pet store will be able to tell you which guinea pigs are males and which are females. Males will grow slightly bigger than females. Males like attention from people and are often more ready to play than females are. Females take longer to get used to new places, but females still make wonderful pets.

Unless you plan to breed guinea pigs, buy either two males or two females. Two guinea pigs that grow up together become close friends.

Guinea pigs enjoy being together. You will often see them sitting close together or even feeding from the same bowl.

Making Friends

Guinea pigs are shy animals and will be nervous in a new home.

When you bring your guinea pigs home, you probably will want to play with them right away, but try to be patient. The guinea pigs first need time to explore their new home and get used to their new surroundings. You can put food in the hutch or cage, but the guinea pigs may not be ready to eat right away.

Handling

When your guinea pigs seem relaxed and happy in their new surroundings, you can start to handle them. If you hold them gently, guinea pigs will become used to you and will enjoy being stroked and cuddled in your lap.

The correct way to hold a guinea pig is to get a firm grasp under its chest with one hand and support the weight of its rear end with the other hand. Sit on

It may take some time, but if you are gentle and patient, your guinea pig will learn to trust you.

the floor when you play with your guinea pigs. These little animals move very quickly, and you do not want your pets to fall if they wriggle out of your hands.

Giving Treats

The way to a guinea pig's heart is through its stomach. Guinea pigs love tasty treats, such as slices of carrots or apples. Give your guinea pigs some of their favorite foods, and they will soon be eating from your fingers. Remember to be quiet when you are around your guinea pigs. Loud noises frighten these little animals. Try to find a time each day when you hand-feed your guinea pigs, and you will soon be a welcome visitor.

Introductions

Guinea pigs are friendly animals, so introducing a newcomer to a group of guinea pigs will not cause any trouble. Put out plenty of food and put the new guinea pig in with the others early in the day. Your guinea pigs will then have time to get to know each other before they go to bed at night.

A guinea pig will not struggle if you hold it the correct way.

Cavy Care

You may see a rabbit sharing a home with guinea pigs, but it is not a good idea. Rabbits have different needs and may bully the guinea pigs.

Healthy Eating

Guinea pigs are not fussy eaters, but they still need a suitable diet.

A guinea pig must have the correct balance of **nutrients** in its diet to grow, stay healthy, and fight disease. Every guinea pig needs four kinds of foods.

- Hay
- Water
- Cereals
- Green and root vegetables

Hay

The wild ancestors of guinea pigs spent all day grazing on grass and plants, and pet guinea pigs are still grazing animals. In fact, guinea pigs find it very hard to digest their food unless they eat plenty of hay. Make sure some high-quality hay, such as Timothy hay, is always available in the hutch or cage.

Feed your guinea pig a bowl of cereal and vegetables once a day.

Water

Like all animals, guinea pigs need fresh, clean water.

Cereals

At the pet store, you can buy a cereal mix that has been specially prepared for guinea pigs. The mix will contain crushed oats, wheat, barley, some form of corn, and grass pellets.

Fruits and Vegetables

Most small animals make their own vitamin C, but, like human beings, guinea pigs do not. Every day, your guinea pigs should eat some fresh fruits and vegetables that contain vitamin C. Kale, cabbage, melons, and apples are good foods, but be sure to remove the apple seeds because they are poisonous to guinea pigs. Guinea pigs also like cauliflower and brussels sprouts, and they enjoy eating dandelion leaves.

Guinea pigs need to gnaw to keep their teeth in good order, so give them some hard root vegetables, such as carrots, turnips, and parsnips.

Fruits and vegetables are important parts of a guinea pig's diet. Hand-feeding your pets can be fun.

Cavy Care

If guinea pigs do not eat enough fruits and vegetables, they may get a condition called scurvy. Scurvy is very painful and can kill them. Scurvy is easily prevented if you provide the right diet.

Guinea Pig Care

When you give guinea pigs a home, you become responsible for all their needs.

If you keep two guinea pigs, their hutch or cage will quickly become dirty with droppings and food remains. Your job is to keep the cage clean.

Daily Tasks

Do the following every day.

- Collect leftover food
- Refill the water bottle
- Clean the feeding bowls
- Remove wet wood chips and droppings

Weekly Tasks

Once a week, remove all the bedding so you can give your guinea pigs a fresh, clean bed. Put your guinea pigs in their playpen or outdoor run while you are busy.

Guinea pigs like a bed of hay, where they can be warm and cozy.

Monthly Tasks

Once a month, scrub your guinea pig's cage or hutch with **disinfectant**. A good pet store will supply you with a disinfectant that is safe for animals.

Grooming

Smooth-haired guinea pigs do not need grooming. Long-haired guinea pigs need some help keeping their coats free from mats and tangles.

If you have a long-haired or Abyssinian guinea pig, you need to start grooming it when it is very young so the guinea pig learns to relax. A baby's toothbrush is ideal for grooming a guinea pig's coat.

Teeth

Pet guinea pigs do not gnaw as much as their wild ancestors, and sometimes, their teeth grow too long. If you see your guinea pig drooling or struggling to eat, it may need to have its teeth clipped. Take your guinea pig to a veterinarian for this job.

After a guinea pig gets used to being groomed, it seems to enjoy the attention.

Cavy Care

Remember that an outside run or a playpen also needs to be kept clean and tidy.

Nails

If you keep your guinea pig on soft bedding, its nails will not wear down and will need to be clipped. Ask your veterinarian or an experienced guinea pig keeper to clip the nails for you.

Cavy Behavior

Watch your guinea pigs closely to find out how they show their feelings.

Guinea Pig Poses

A guinea pig's body position is often a clue to how the guinea pig feels.

Lying Stretched Out

A relaxed, contented guinea pig will stretch out.

Stiff-legged Trotting

If you have two male guinea pigs, and one trots around with stiff legs, he is trying to be the boss.

Mating Dance

Male guinea pigs hop and wriggle in front of females that are ready for breeding.

Jumping

When a guinea pig is in high spirits, it will suddenly jump from a standstill. This jumping is known as "popcorning."

Touching Noses

Friendly guinea pigs greet each other by touching noses.

Standing on Hind Legs

Guinea pigs standing on hind legs are angry and ready to fight.

Freezing

A guinea pig will suddenly stand still if it hears a loud or unfamiliar sound or sees something that it thinks looks scary.

Did You Know?

If a guinea pig sees an enemy and is very frightened, it will lie on its back, completely still. The guinea pig is pretending to be dead so the enemy will go away.

A mother guinea pig will often coo to her piglets.

Guinea Pig Chatter

Guinea pigs use coos, squeaks, chatters, chortles, and chirps to "talk" to each other. When your guinea pigs are comfortable with you, they will talk to you, too.

All the sounds that guinea pigs make have their own special meanings.

Coos

Your guinea pig is content when it is cooing. A mother guinea pig coos to her babies, and sometimes, a guinea pig will also coo to its owner.

Squeaks

When a guinea pig has been hurt or is very upset, it will give a high-pitched squeak. Sometimes, young guinea pigs give this squeak when they miss their mothers. Squeaks are also used to warn other guinea pigs of danger.

Chatters

An angry guinea pig will chatter its teeth to tell other guinea pigs to stay away. If a guinea pig is roughly treated, it may chatter at its human handler.

Chortles

A throaty chuckle shows that a guinea pig is relaxed and happy. You may hear this sound when you are stroking your guinea pig.

Wheeeek!

Guinea pigs say "wheek" when they see that food is on its way. Some guinea pigs will make this sound when they hear a bag rustle or even when the refrigerator door is opened!

Glossary

allergic: having a reaction to certain substances like animal fur that results in health problems, such as breathing difficulties or skin disorders

ancestor: a relative from the distant past

boar: a male guinea pig

cavies: another name for guinea pigs

crossbred: describes animals that are produced by parents of different varieties

disinfectant: a chemical cleaner that kills germs

graze: to feed on growing plants

Incas: an ancient people who lived in Peru, a country in South America

incisors: front teeth for biting

mammals: warm-blooded animals that give birth to live young

marked: a guinea pig whose coat is a combination of colors

nutrients: substances in food that keep animals healthy

predators: hunters

pregnancy: the condition of a female carrying unborn offspring inside her body

primary colors: the three basic colors that create all the other colors

purebred: describes an animal produced by a male and female of the same recognized breed

rodent: a group of mammals that have four big front teeth that are used for gnawing

sacrificed: killed during a ceremony as an offering to gods

self-colored: a guinea pig whose coat is one color

sows: female guinea pigs

More Books to Read

101 Facts About Guinea Pigs
Julia Barnes
(Gareth Stevens)

**Getting To Know Your
Guinea Pig**
Gill Page
(TFH Publications)

Guinea Pig
Looking After My Pet (series)
David Alderton
(Lorenz Books)

I Love Guinea Pigs
Read and Wonder (series)
Dick King-Smith
(Candlewick Press)

My Guinea Pig and Me
Immanuel Birmelin
(Barron's Educational)

Web Sites

Beanmakers: Guinea Pig and Cavy Lovers Heaven
beanmakers.com

Guinea Pig Breeds
www.comfycavies.com/Info/Breeds/breeds.htm

Guinea Pig Play
cavycages.com/toys.htm

Publisher's note to educators and parents: Our editors have carefully reviewed these Web sites to ensure that they are suitable for children. Many Web sites change frequently, however, and we cannot guarantee that a site's future contents will continue to meet our high standards of quality and educational value. Be advised that children should be closely supervised whenever they access the Internet.

Index